Daughter of a Vietnam Veteran

Leiloni Lynn Caughell-Simpson

Dedication

Dedicated to my father—a Vietnam Veteran.

Leiloni Lynn Caughell-Simpson

About the Author

Reliving the past as I did was quite a relief. I got to let the readers know about my childhood. I grew up in Shelton, Washington State, and lived in the same spot until I was twenty -nine. Then, I moved to Taylor, Michigan, where I reside now.

Growing up had its ups and downs, but I grew from them. I lost my dad when I was twenty-eight and lived in Washington for a couple of months after that.

My dad was my world, so I decided to write about the life we had together. Every once in a while, I'd have a flashback of the times me and Dad spent together and would write them down as they came. They came with joy and sadness.

Diagnosed with PTSD at nineteen, I delt with the flashbacks all alone until I decided to write this book. Now, I live with my best friend and a dog named Harbor. They keep me going.

Living with PTSD is hard at times, but my dog helps me out of my horrifying flashbacks.

Daughter of a Veitnam Veteran

I love hiking, enjoying water of any kind, finding new things, and going to yard sales on the side.

Summers are my favorite time of year, but sometimes, you get burnt. That is certainly no fun.

The creator helps me be wise and in an abundance of creation, and the way to live life with the creatures and the trees.

Here's to hoping you guys who have picked up this book to read and will enjoy it and its treasures.

Leiloni Lynn Caughell-Simpson

Table of Contents

Dedication...i

About the Author ii

Preface vi

Chapter One..1

Ambushing the Enemy 1

Chapter Two 13

Learning to be a Soldier 13

Chapter Three 23

The Christmas Decorations 23

Chapter Four..31

Into the Water We Go! 31

Chapter Five 43

Burried Alive 43

Chapter Six...52

Anabelle...52

Chapter Seven...63

The Seizure...63

Chapter Eight 71

The Mitsubishi 71

Chapter Nine 81

The Cool Parents.. 81

Chapter Ten 96

My Dad, My Hero!.. 96

Preface

The outlook on *"Daughter of a Vietnam Veteran"* to me, and the walk of life of such a man.

My father looked like a sasquatch and even talked like him, too. He was well known for being the greatest man around. He cared about a lot of people, and those people will always be remembered by him, even in the afterlife.

Running the club and being the president of the *Vietnam Veterans Bike Club* were his waking moments when he was clean and sober.

Drugs have taken a lot of men from the Vietnam War, but not taken the hearts of those men.

They fought for our country forever. It was different being raised by a man like him, but he never gave up on me. Even in his old age, he tried to keep up with me and did as I did.

This book is about the life that we went through, the two of us against the world.

The stories that can cripple a country in just moments if lived by the life of a Vietnam veteran, but he raised a daughter in the most exquisite way.

Daughter of a Veitnam Veteran

The stories told in this book are very true and very vivid like you are living them yourself.

I bring you the story of a daughter of a Vietnam veteran. May the moon be at your back and the sun on your face.

Leiloni Lynn Caughell-Simpson

Blank Page Left Intentionally

Chapter One

Ambushing the Enemy

"Wake up! There's something creeping around here! Shh! Be very quiet. The enemy is outside. Listen very closely so you can hear them. Remember, at least one soldier must always be by my side." Came the sounds of a disabled, crazed veteran.

"I'm up! What do you mean they are outside?" I asked, confused.

With a loaded pistol in his hand, Dad reaches out and puts his hand over my mouth. "Shh, I told you they are outside. You ready to take down the enemy?" He asked.

"No, Dad, I'm tired. I'm going back to sleep." I answered.

Shaking his head frantically, Dad pulls me off the bed and gets a crazy look in his eyes and on his bearded face.

"No! You are coming with me!" He orders me.

"Fine, Dad. Where is he?" I asked, irritated.

"He? You mean the enemy?" He corrected me.

"Yes, I mean the enemy," I replied.

"Okay, let's scout them," Dad said excitedly.

"Here we go! It's going to be a long ride and a long night. Where you at, you little pricks? My daughter and I are going to scout you out and kill your ugly asses! This is war! We fight, we light, and it's gonna go all night! You, this is my rifle. This is my gun! We're gonna find you because you are number one! He shouted.

Then, he runs over to the cabinet in the house and says, "Get over here. We're at war."

Then, he continues, "Listen to the sounds of the night. Is there anything you don't recognize? What sounds can you hear?"

"I hear that one. Oh, yeah, that one. One, two, three, he comes with me. Crazy at night and brave during the day. Listen to what I say. Light the night and broaden the day. Listen to what I say. One, two, it is you! Three, four, I hear the door. Don't mess with me cause, five, four, that's a whore! Off task is the bearded stash. Seven, eight—we skipped six, so now you're late!" Dad booms.

"I hear the enemy at the side. This is the ride. Hey, fuckers, I got a bomb!"

Kaboom! The grenade goes out the door.

"Shh, I think I got them. Let's go see what we got. This will be fun."

Dad laughs. "There's a devil on the ground. Damn, the grenade didn't get them. That's okay. We have dinner tonight. A fox."

Then he walks inside with his prize that he had gotten and says, "Mmm... A fox for dinner. You better be hungry."

"I'm gonna have a lot of personal stuff spilling out, so you better get a box of tissues and grab a bag of popcorn, too. The deadly roller coaster ride. Hold on, soldiers! Don't give up!" He says.

"He's at our viewpoint! Don't let him out of sight!" With his loaded shotgun in his hand, he crawls like a snake on the ground. Well, the two of us did, me and him.

He whispers to his right shoulder, "You see how he's right there?"

"Yes, Daddy, he's right there," I whisper back.

"Right there!" He exclaims.

"Yes, Dad."

"Now, sshh. We gotta be quiet. We're coming up on his backside. Don't make any noise." He hands me the gun.

Then, he yelled. "Three, four is a bearded whore!"

And I take aim.

"Get them, sissy." He orders, and I load off on them.

"Get them, sissy! You got it!" I fired the gun just like he wanted and hit the damn thing.

"Another fox for dinner. I say you did pretty good. Now, that's how you raise a daughter." He says proudly.

First shot, and she lands it! Golly! She's my daughter for sure." He says proudly as he grabs the dead animal from the shooting range.

"Come on, baby girl, we're having Fox for dinner tonight."

We walk back to the homestead and see Mamma there on the porch, waiting for us.

Daughter of a Veitnam Veteran

"God, you must have good ears to know we were on the way to ya. The second fox of the week," he says to Mamma.

The one time she's home and I land a fox!

"By golly, she did well. Better than I'd ever be, and that says a lot. I mean it. I'm a dead shot. Must run through our blood." He lays the fox on our porch.

The smell of fox cooking while you're on red alert with your dad, sounds mighty tasty, but it's worth it with this item for a tasty dinner. As he would say.

This is how we lived the days of our lives. Crazy, chaotic, and always happening—never a dull moment to rest.

I don't know if my dad is the worst case, but I do know that he definitely was a crazy guy. So crazy that you would never suspect the love that he truly had deep inside his heart.

The flashbacks come in and out of the traumatic life of a Vietnam veteran. So many stories to tell you. Stuff you wouldn't believe going on to the soldiers of that brutal war. What they went through and what they brought home with them.

My father had so much love to give and got so much love in return. Everyone who knew him loved him. I mean, the guy had around five-hundred friends when he died. Our family was pretty big, too, and everyone loved him.

He always wanted to have someone sit down and write his story out. So, that's why I'm writing this to tell my outlook on his life and the fun, crazy, off-the-wall shit that man put me through too.

For instance, he woke me up at the craziest times and had me be his own personal soldier. One that he could rely on and *kill the enemy* with.

Dad and I were best friends. There's a lot of stuff that I wish I could write, but it would be treason for me. So, as the memories of a little girl rush through my head, I grab the fun and funny stuff. Things you'd want to hear about.

My dad taught me everything I know, and I can't believe how he did it! But in the end, I came out pretty strong from all the shit he put me through. I learned a lot of lessons from him. Holding a shotgun is one of them.

He gave me my own pistol to guard the house with when he was gone, and we'd play in the dark.

Daughter of a Veitnam Veteran

He'd creep through the night, and I'd make him my mark target.

Once, I remember him being so drunk that he even put the barrel of the gun to his head and said, "Shoot me."

"No, Daddy, I won't do it," I answered.

"Shoot me! I mean it! Your mother is gone. I have no food. I'm out of ammo. You're the only one with ammo, and that's the next guy's shot!" He insisted.

I shook my head in denial again.

"Never mind. I'll take the gun from you, and I'll actually use it! Use it just for fun, you grumble. I'll actually use it! You could have killed me when you had the chance. Now, I will kill you!" He said.

Just then, we heard someone at the door. Dad turned around, and my uncle walked in.

"Oh, thank god, it's you!" Dad said

I release the breath I didn't even know I was holding in.

"Yeah, Lonny, it's me." My uncle answered.

Dad sloshed around some more, raised the gun, and shot it off in the air.

"Damn, Lonny, you're gonna kill somebody with that shit! Be fucking careful!" My uncle yelled.

But thank God no one accidentally got shot.

So, that's to share how Dad was. Always running around with a gun or a knife. I guess it was from the war? I could never fully comprehend or understand it.

He was in the first infantry division. So, he was on the ground and always was with a weapon. I think that is the reason he loved his weapon more than anything else in the world. Even sex wasn't interesting for him. While he slept, his weapon was always at his side, too. With Dad, you always felt protected!

He had guerrilla warfare down to a T, and also, with his weapon and wife, there was the feeling of a very sheltered and secure home.

Once, we got invited to a *get-together* out in Matlock, Washington.

"Hey, how are you doing today? Haven't seen you in a while. You're cooking up some of your special salmon. Mmm, it smells good." Dad praised.

"Been cooking it all night?" He asked and sniffed some more.

"You know I have, Lonny. That's the way you make them." Answered Dad's buddy, who was cooking the fish, as he flipped it.

"Well, you hungry, little one?" Dad said to me.

"Yeah, Daddy, I'm hungry," I answered, rubbing my tummy childishly.

"Well, give me one of your famous fish filets," Dad said to his friend.

The guy reached out, flipped the fish on a plate, and handed Dad the plate, and we walked away.

The blues played in the background, and Dad started jamming to the song out loud. He dips low with his body and feels the music in his structure. The blues always did me right. My uncle used to listen to it all the time, so I was always a *blues* baby. God, it feels so good to just let the music play in your bones.

My mom had made us flower headbands for our heads, and we were wearing them. Annabella and I put them on and started dancing around to the music.

My mom was twisting and twirling with the music, and Annabella and I danced and twirled with each other. We let the music play our every move, dancing to it and jamming out.

Out of the corner of my eye, I see Dad sitting in the grass and cheering us on.

"Woohoo! You go, baby girls and Momma!" He cheered us on.

He was always so proud of us. Always loved us and was a really good guy. The best man I've ever known. No matter what it was, he was always behind us, being our cheerleader.

Like this one time, I was doing the dishes, and he walked in and was like, "Mhm, my baby girl, you certainly are doing pretty good at that. Where'd you learn it from?"

"You, of course, daddy." I laughed.

"Thank God, I taught you well, little missy. Because I've seen some ratchet girls out there, and they're trying to land a guy without a dish in hand or some kind of dishwashing skills or plating skills." He said, quite seriously, might I add.

"No, huh, uh, they don't do a dish nor nothing. They'll go to their grave with not a dish in hand. Makes me think of something... Hmm... Should I bury a girl with a dish in her hand? Should I?" Dad asked, again, quite seriously.

"No, Daddy, that'd be too much, and you don't want to go to jail over no dish in a woman's hand." I laughed.

Now, I admit that he was not always the brightest tool in a tool shed, but he did say some crazy shit sometimes. It was hard to grasp where he even came up with this shit! Burying some lady with a dish in her hand to make a point or something? He was definitely one of a kind.

My father. My hero. The war really fucked him up, but he was still my father. And to be honest, I believe he was one of the best ones out there.

What do you think? Was he a crazy guy? Was he a tough guy? What was he? Ladies, would you go for a guy who tells you he'd bury you if you don't do the dishes or set the table? With a dish at that?

Cheering me on in his own way, I guess? Making me feel special the way he wants to at that. Men. Or is it just Vietnam veterans? I don't know, but it made me feel good. Like his commenting on me was paying attention to me. And I loved the attention I got from my father. So, in a weird way. I like his comments.

Chapter Two

Learning to be a Soldier

"Daddy, I wove you!" I said in my childish tone.

"I wove you too, my little bundle of fur!" He said, putting on fox fur and getting all bundled up by the fire.

"Going on a mission. We go to the sternums of the wood, fire, and safety bin!" He goes as we start our mission to the wood pile. One leg in front of the other. Snow as tall as my waist.

"Come on, baby. You can do it!" He cheered on me, as always.

One foot in front of the other. Come on! We're going over the snow and to the woods to grandmother's house! Off we go! To get the wood and stack it up. To grandmother's house, we go!" He chanted.

"Almost there." He concluded.

Then he pointed in the direction of a heap.

Leiloni Lynn Caughell-Simpson

"You see that, little soldier? It's a snow pile. Now get down and crouch."

"I see ya! We're coming up on you. You better look out." He said as if there was an enemy there.

At that very moment, an eagle swarmed in on us.

Dad said, "It's the eagle's nest. Dive, dive! Run, baby. Run!" And we ran to the woodshed.

"Run as fast as your little legs will rise up and down." He said, chuckling. He was enjoying this. And seeing him chuckle like that filled my heart with this warm feeling, and I started chuckling too.

"Grab your wood now, little one." He laughed to himself.

"Grab your wood. Hold out your arms." He instructed, and I held out my arms.

"Yeah, like that. That's right. Now we're going to stack the wood on top of each other." He said and put one in my arms.

"One, two, three! Here ya go, baby girl. Now hopefully, you can make it through that snow with all that lovely wood to start a fire with." He smiled.

Then, he filled up his own arms, "And daddy's Gotta grab his load now." He says.

"Now, we're headed home. Come on, come on. Over the piles of snow, one foot in front of the other. Now come on!" He laughed.

Going through the snow was cold and clumsy. I'm lucky I didn't drop a log one. I kept it straight and lifted my legs up as high as they went.

Swoosh! Squish! Squash!

I would have fallen if I hadn't had the snow to keep me balanced. I mean, this snow was pretty deep for a five-year-old. Two feet of snow. That was a blessing in itself because I wouldn't have been praised as much as I was by my dad if the snow hadn't helped me stay upright.

He was really giving me props. "You got it, baby! It's gonna be okay."

"You're too cute trying to manage that pile of snow we got last night. Now come on. Up the steps we go!"

And finally, we made it.

"Woohoo! You made it! Congratulations. I love you!"

"Now, put the wood in the stove." I did as instructed.

"Nice, we have a fire now." Dad sighed contentedly like he had accomplished the world.

It was always like this with him. The smallest things made him the happiest.

Daddy was always on an adventure with me. No matter what it was, it was an adventure! Getting wood to keep us warm, now that's some nature skills you got to have. That was his thinking.

One more of the many things I learned from my father was that you have to know how to make a fire and get wood for that fire. You have to have the technique to make fire! Because if you're lost in the woods, and you are cold, and it's the dead of winter, in which you don't know how to make a fire, then you're shit out of luck. You'd die if you didn't know how to make fire, being lost and all that stuff.

So, I will give you some advice. It doesn't take long and is pretty easy once you get it down. It's like riding a bike or being physically intimate. You'll always know how. Like I said, go out and do it now! Set aside a day to learn how to make fire! It'll be the best damn thing you will ever do. I promise!

All that good stuff... I can't believe I carried that much wood at such a young age. Giving myself props because that's how me and Dad stayed warm. With time, I got used to it. Gathering firewood for the fire was an everyday thing. My Dad and I trampled through the snow. We had to have a fire somehow.

There were many times we breached the snow. I fell a couple times, and I dropped the wood so many times.

Then, when Dad noticed this, he started not taking me out because we had to have a fire quickly, and I slowed him down.

"Daddy, what are you doing? I thought you needed help?" I'd say.

"No, baby, I got this."

"Okay, Daddy, I wove you." I would say in my baby voice.

"I wove you too, my precious sunshine." He would mimic me.

"Through all of this snow, I go." And off he would go.

Day by day, the snow would melt, but then it would snow again, and it would all be the same. We had blizzards and storms. You name it, we had it.

One time, it snowed so much that the trees went heavy. Then, the wind came. You could hear the trees cracking and snapping. It was a total mess. We even had to watch the trees that were close to the house go through the same.

"It's a storm brewing. Watch out for those widow makers. You can hear them snapping." My dad yelled as we trampled through the snow. The windowmakers are trees that are leaning on other trees that are dead and alive. You come across them in the woods.

They come either way. Dead leaning on an alive tree and alive leaning on a dead tree. These can break and fall right on you or a house. So, they call them windowmakers. It's a logging term that the loggers use when they're cutting down trees in the woods. You definitely don't want it to happen.

My mom was scared, "Watch that tree over there."

"Oh, it's a tough house. I built it! It's gonna hold no matter what hits us. This house is sturdy." Dad answered.

Then he pointed in the other direction. "We'll have to cut fall those ones over there. I'll get my chainsaw. We'll take 'em down. Just hope I'm right on the heavy side. Don't want to hurt myself. Or better yet, kill myself." He laughed.

And yes, he cut that tree that day and didn't get hurt or kill himself. It was scary, but with my dad by my side, it was overcoming. I trusted my dad every time he made a decision after that. He was my superhero.

Now, as I'm about to turn thirty- two, I relive all those moments I spent with my dad, and my heart fills with this inexplainable warmth. Dad would have been sixty-two this coming up, January 25th. Yep, in 1951. He was born on a snowy winter's day.

I remember he used to tell me about his adventures through the woods and driving here to Washington State from Minnesota. He narrated how the heater didn't work, and there were no seatbelts. Dad talked about how the car wasn't made like the cars on the road today.

All made out of tin, not Steele. Cars would wreck, and you'd be saved by the car. But there were no seatbelts.

"It was like a boat!" He would exclaim. "Like a big old boat floating on water." Well, at least that's how he saw it.

He reminisced how his dad drove the whole way, only stopping a few times. In the snow, they came. All four of his brothers and sisters. Traveling to a new state.

Just on a whim to get a job because there was no work for his dad back home. So, onto a new awakening, new scenery, new home, new everything.

He was the middle child and a stubborn old mule at that. Had to be born an Aquarius! We were like milk and soda. One bubbly and the other soft and sweet.

And in that way, I was exactly like Daddy. Both of us were the same. I'm sure he'd get into arguments with his mom and Dad, seeing how I would. We would fight like cats and dogs.

Round and round again. "Daddy, please!" I'd say.

"No!" Would come his booming response.

"Come on, please?" I would plead.

"No!" He would boom again.

"But you said yes!" I would then try to trick him.

Daughter of a Veitnam Veteran

"No, I never said yes." He would answer.

"You did! Right there! Come on, please? You said yes. You have to when you already said yes. Come on, you promised!" I would whine.

"No, I did not." He would stay on his point.

It would go on for hours until I got my way. That's how he said yes to braces.

"I had to have them, or I would be a loser. They'd make fun of me." That's what I told him.

"She has her dad wrapped around my little finger." My mom would always say, with a jealous tone.

Always so jealous. I hated that about my mom. Why was she so upset about our relationship? How could you even be jealous of your own flesh and blood?

I mean, okay, I can see it. The way that you lose your puppy love when a baby comes into the picture. It becomes a pack, not a one-on-one.

So, the ladies that have jealousy, it's okay. We will always love you. You're our mom. How can you lose that feeling?

Leiloni Lynn Caughell-Simpson

I mean, as a daughter of a jealous mother, my love for her never became any less. And that is why it was one of the hardest times for me, losing her to alcohol.

I still love her the same to this day. That love will always be her, right in my heart. That, I know and am sure of.

Chapter Three

The Christmas Decorations

My dad loved his mother a lot. That's for sure. His mom was his life. But sadly, she passed away because of breast cancer back in the 80s. Then her husband followed after.

They say he died of a broken heart. The two of them had five kids together and moved here from Minnesota. They say raising one kid is tough. But imagine raising five. That, in itself, is the makings of a strong woman and a strong relationship.

Imagine the bond you'd have with your wife. You'd love her to the grave like that. She would be your hero. Building a strong relationship would be hard, but he had to daydream about her as she handled all those kids and took care of dinner.

The dinner was made with love but only from a piece of bread and some kidney beans, like in that movie where Mickey Mouse and his friends have only one bean and have to cut it into little slices and share.

Pretty amazing, isn't it? They had to have all kinds of memories together. If I had someone that close to me, I'd surely die of a broken heart too.

So, in his mother's memory, my dad kept the Christmas bulbs she used all those years she was with him. Dad had them all lined up in a secure box. Well, according to him, it was a secure box, but the damn dog or cat would break one every year.

So, keeping the tradition, which, of course, fell onto me after him, I saved all my Christmas stuff, and I even found bulbs that looked just like hers, and I kept them sacred in my home too.

No one is allowed to break them, and I'm keeping them till I am sixty. No joke! My kids need to have some memories too. And that is why, this Christmas, those sacred bulbs lit up the room.

I wish I still had some of the Christmas stuff my dad had saved. But then I will have to venture out to Shelton, Washington. Then, I would have to get up in the attic and sort through all the stuff up there. But that's not the biggest obstacle. The problem is that I live in Michigan now, and I can't fly just for the Christmas stuff.

Daughter of a Veitnam Veteran

Everybody in the family has their own thing going on, and half of them do not even live in Washington anymore. But yeah, it is definitely on my bucket list. To gallivant to Washington and get the Christmas decorations.

I remember once, at home, which was in the middle of nowhere, my raising grounds, where I grew up, I was looking for my dad because it was too quiet. I saw his legs lying out of a big heap of brush, the Salal.

I mean, no one lived out there but us for miles. We had to cross the water to get out to civilization in the winter until spring when the river beads would dry up. It was definitely an unusual part of my life.

We didn't have running water, no well, no electricity, no sewer. But my dad, he had made his own setup.

We used to think, "What is this man even thinking?"

But whatever he did, it always worked. Thank God for a generator! That thing couldn't run a hair straightener, but it aided us in having light. No one wants to live in the dark if you know what I mean!

He did the Einstein type of stuff. He would make out of little light bulbs and wires. It turned out to be exactly like the light contraption you make in school. The light bulb, a battery, a plate of metal, and some wires. Yep, that contraption. It was pretty cool how he had it set up.

The generator could run the whole house. It was amazing. And in this house of mysteries resided my sister, mom, Dad, and I. A three-bedroom, one-bath home that was built from a manufactured home. A single but wide trailer.

He added onto it room by room and finished it pretty fast. He had help from all my uncles and my older sister, Teresa, but mostly, it was him. But yes, having had all that help made Dad's life a lot easier. It was a lot easier to manage and maintain on a room-by-room basis.

Also, it was pretty cool to watch and be able to learn the makeup of a house. Learning the layout of what's inside the walls and how to make a house come together, Dad makes it look so fun.

Then, there were all kinds of animals that would hang out around the house. Foxes, snakes, frogs, lizards, mice, rats, bears, and coyotes. I'd go on my own missions finding new things and playing with the old. Frogs were the coolest for me. Looking mighty green and sometimes brown—and we had toads too.

Daughter of a Veitnam Veteran

So, back to the story, Dad was doing some outside work. You know, working on the house. The one he had been putting together, and all of a sudden, I found a tree frog!

And, of course, my discovery was something I needed to show Dad. Dad had to see.

"Hey, Daddy! Look what I found! A Froggy!" I told him excitedly.

"Then you need a home, indeed." He replied.

"But where can we find a home for it?"

He pretended to think for a while, then jumped, "Oh, I have just the thing for it!"

"Hey guys, I'm going to find a jar for my kid." He informed the rest.

"Now, you, little one, follow me. I have got just the thing for this."

He kept talking as he looked around. "Okay, well, it's not here. Maybe it's over there. Oh, here we go. Just the thing! A jar for your froggy. You can keep him as your own pet.

But just wait. You gotta put the lid on it. But also, you don't want the poor thing to suffocate, now, do you?"

"Watch this. You take the lid to the jar and stab holes through it. Then you put the frog in the jar and tighten the lid on it."

Putting the frog in the jar, he said, "Now, you gotta have some grass and a twig in there too, so he has something to stand on. This will keep him safe. Better air for him."

Reaching down, he then grabbed a handful of grass and put it in the jar with the frog.

"Now a twig. Let's find a twig. He will like that. Oh, yes, he will like that." Dad went on.

"There we go. Right there. Can you grab it for me?" Dad asked me.

"No, can you grab it for me? Please, Dad. I don't want to grab the wrong one." I answered, scared to mess up.

"Okay, baby." He said as he bent over and picked it up.

"Open the jar and do it slowly so he doesn't escape," Dad instructed me.

Opening the jar very slowly, he then slipped the stick in there with the frog.

After that, for two or three days, I kept that frog in the jar. Everywhere I'd go. the poor thing went with me.

Then one day, I went to find my frog, and it wasn't in the jar.

"Mom? Dad? Have you seen my frog?" I panicked.

"No, baby!" Dad yells from the back room.

"It didn't need to be in the jar, anyway." Came my mother's answer. "You know they can escape through little tiny holes, don't you?"

"No, really, momma?"

"Yes, baby." And she went into the house.

Now, I know that she probably threw it out, but then, I believed that frogs could escape through tiny holes. That was something I believed my whole childhood.

I still think maybe they can because mice can fit through any hole that their head can fit through.

Leiloni Lynn Caughell-Simpson

So maybe she wasn't lying. I never got to ask her about that ever again. It just never came up in conversation.

Chapter Four

Into the Water We Go!

As I mentioned earlier, we had to cross the water to go to civilization.

Voom! Going through the water over the roadway, it was quite a journey.

We had this little Toyota pickup, a red one at that. The vehicle that lasted us for years. I think it lasted us ten to twelve years, but that's just gravy. It might have lasted long, but we sure did put it through some shit.

"Hold onto your britches! This is going to be a sure ride if we don't drift away." Dad hollered to us as we drove past the river.

"Sure, looks like we can clear it. Let's put this baby to work." He mumbled.

Vroom! Went that Toyota motor. Straight in the middle, separating the body of water in two.

"We can make it! We gonna make it!" He opened the Toyota door and, swish! Went the water. It looked like we were in the middle of a river.

"Oh shit! We're getting deeper." He shut the door.

"Oh, damn, baby! Are we going to make it?"

"Come on, baby! We're going to make it." But the water was now up to the car window, almost through it.

"Damn, baby, we made it!" Dad exclaimed as we came out the other side.

"I hope we can make it through on our way back. We're probably going to have to park it and walk in." He said.

So, we made it to school. "Thank God, this baby made it. I just knew she could." That was a crazy lake expo. Dad sure knew how to drive. He surely did. He was a good driver. We actually made it, and that was a close one.

The school was very fun that day. I surely was scared when that water was up to the window. It wasn't quite enough to go over the hood of the car, but it almost surely did.

But my day was quite eventful as I got to tell all my friends the story of the ordeal that I had gone through that following morning.

And even though it was a good day at school, if the water had gone over the hood of the car, we would've been stuck swimming out of that overgrown sinkhole. And then, I would've been pissed! Getting my school clothes wet.

Oh no. You definitely don't want that response out of me. I would've cried and had a silly downward smile on my face. You know, the look of a puppy kind of thing. I would have pouted and would have been upset, and Dad wouldn't have let that happen. He surely wouldn't have. And then I would have gotten out of going to school that day. No throwing a tantrum and having a cow this time.

"No daughter of mine would have to go through all that! Nope." He'd say.

I just know if it would have happened, it would've been bad. But, thank God, it didn't happen like that, and we got through that *heap in the road.*

Living with my dad had its ups and downs. He'd be all there sometimes and be in the war zone the next. We surely did have a blast, though. He was the most loving person you would have ever met. He would give you the shirt off his back as long as you weren't the enemy. Now if you were the enemy, you would get the shirt, but as soon as you put it on, he'd have your neck and probably break it.

So, I was the enemy a couple times. It was scary. If he was past the fun mode, I stayed out of his way because he did have the whip. His belt would strike me because I was the enemy. It was quite scary.

The look in his eyes was so cold. I mean cold, but on fire at the same time. Like looking someone dead in the eye and seeing death is going to be happening here shortly and fire burning deep in his soul at the same time.

It was a startling look. Death be to the enemy! Death be. But me? I would look even deeper and find my dad. At the bottom, I swear. And I'm not allowed to swear unless it's a cuss word because that means war. So, you know I'm telling the truth. I swear!

It was scary at night. And I mean it, actually scary.

Once, Dad left us, and we were hiding in the bushes. We were on high alert. Dad came outside to check on something moving in the bushes, and bam! We hid our asses off. Hiding in the shadows.

"Hiding from the big bad wolf, are you? You got your gun because I do, little missies. Do you think you can hide from an A-1 soldier like me? I guess not." He laughed.

"Aha! I found you!" He did a turn toward my sister.

"I got you, little one!" Dangling her from her feet on his back.

"No, Daddy, no! Oh, no!" Was her response.

"You're just for bate. I got me a slithering snake."

Me? I immediately gilded from one shadow to the next.

"As quiet as a mouse, are we? Yep, there's our little mouse." Dad shot off a round, barely missing me.

"But I missed, oh, shit."

Grabbing the opportunity, I ran for the door.

"The little soldier is running for the door!" He yelled, bam, bam!

"I'm missing you, number one. Where's my little soldier going?"

"Away from you," I yelled, and he came up running to me.

"You're my number one. You can't turn on me now. I'd be a mess without you." But I didn't listen and kept running.

"Go, be like your mother." And with that, he went into the house.

There was snow everywhere. I hid in the bushes and got close to a tree to keep me warm. About an hour later, I realized Mom wasn't coming home.

"You have a nice time waiting? Your mother's got a problem, Leiloni. I love you, my darling daughter. Please, don't be like her. Please, don't leave us. Please."

I started crying, and he held me. "I know, I know. I know!" The tone of his voice got louder and louder. "I'll just shut up." He cried.

I fell myself to sleep in his arms. Then, I woke up, and he had a fire going.

"I miss Mom," I mumbled softly.

Daughter of a Veitnam Veteran

"I do, too, baby. I do, too." Came his soft whisper, and he started to cry.

"Why can't she just be the woman she is supposed to be? I mean, she bore them. Why can't she love them? Leave an old crazy guy like me to raise them. Why?" He talked to himself, but I was listening. That day, my heart broke.

Being without a mom was very hard. She left us all alone all the time. Not even caring that her babies were in the arms of a traumatized veteran. I know it was hard, but Dad did do it. He raised me very well if you ask me.

Better than she could have, I guess. Because if there were things he could give, the one, the most important thing was always there. And that was love. He loved us more than anything.

He taught me many things. I always hold the door open for my elders. If there is no seat for someone, I offer mine. Common courtesy, I know.

I am never afraid of anything in life because I have already lived through the worst. I am totally prepared for life and ready to take on the world with both hands.

Once, I remember, my dad got on himself a craze for snakes. He had been trying to get this snake—*the enemy*. He called that.

"Dad, what are you doing?" I asked.

"Shh! The enemy is out." He answered and shushed me.

"What enemy?" I questioned.

But then, suddenly, my world went black. I was unconscious because he stabbed me in the face. Or hit me. I don't know. All I know is that it made me catatonic for a second.

I remember waking up with a terrifying view. Dad had a knife in his mouth and a snake in his hand.

"Don't get in the way of me and my snake. I'm hungry. I haven't eaten in days! Do you want some? I know it's just a little baby snake, but it'll work. Don't you think so? Fried snake, yum!" He said.

Not really the smell of choice if you get it scared, which is hard to do, because it's not the friendliest, smelling little thing. All we had were gardener snakes, and they put out the nastiest smell when you terrify them, which isn't hard to do.

All you have to do is grab them, and they let off this raunchy smell you can't believe. So, a snake, yuck! But it worked for food.

Dad made me try everything he could think of. I mean everything! So, he fried up the snake. It worked out great because the calcium it gave him made him normal again.

'Fried snake. Good in calcium and is a great nutritious snack. Yum!' I thought to myself.

The stuff he did might have been crazy to some, but that was my dad. See, he was crazy, like off his rocker, but I still came out a good person with great qualities. I mean, I never signed up for the army, but I lived like I did. I lived like a soldier.

Dad had PTSD, Post-traumatic stress syndrome. He developed his during his time in the war, and it got worse over time. It was nuts. This happens to people every day.

Sometimes, I think lots of people think that people are crazy, but aren't you crazy too? I know you have secrets that you don't tell anybody. I mean, even priests have been found to be child molesters, and some might say that they are perfect. But the truth is, nothing is perfect.

Leiloni Lynn Caughell-Simpson

There are millions of people, and everyone has their own style, smells, looks, etc. So, you could be perfect to someone but not a bit fruity to someone else. Does this make my Dad crazy, or was he just misunderstood?

I don't know, but it just lingers in the back of my head. Was he really crazy? When I say he was crazy, am I right?

Another episode with him was when he assumed the enemies were on top of us in a helicopter.

"They're on top of us! Leius! What do we do?" He yelled.

"Dad, what's on top of us?" I asked.

"The helicopters! Right up there! Can't you hear them?" He answered, agitated.

"No, Dad, I don't hear them." I tried to calm him.

"Baby, they're right there!" He tried to make me believe him.

"Okay, Daddy." I gave in.

"They are getting louder!" He became more agitated.

"Nothing is there, Daddy. Just calm down, okay?" I tried again.

"I can hear them."

"That's all that matters, Daddy," I said. I closed my eyes and released a long sigh. He had really gone crazy.

"I can't believe you didn't hear that. It was so loud. They were right above us. They were soaring low. I wonder what they were looking for?" Dad said when his episode passed.

But I knew and understood. For him, it was real. Dad went through times when he thought there were helicopters above him. While he lay in his room, he would hear them. Sometimes, they were actually there, but other times, he would be hearing things. Going through flashbacks after flashbacks of the war really messed his mind up.

He wasn't allowed any firearms because he would use them on things that weren't there and could kill someone in a heartbeat. Guerrilla warfare. The deadliest of techniques. When he did have his guns, he would be out in the mud and in the bushes, thinking he was going to kill someone or something.

It was quite funny at times, and we would laugh about how silly Daddy was being. But other times, it was downright scary. Dad was about 5'11. He had a black beard and long curly hair. He was fit and weighed about 250 lbs. He always wore black. Black everything. His pants were black, and his shirts were always black. The shirts had a pocket on the left side. His shoes varied from dark brown sandals to brown knockers.

When he'd ride his Harley, he'd wear his riding boots. So, he looked like a black-bearded Santa Claus. His other accessory was a beer in his hand. When he was riding his Harley, he would wear his leather jacket and chaps. Chaps were leather pants with the butt cut out and a slit down the side. They'd keep his legs warm but let some air in too.

He sounded like this, *'Grumble, grumble, I, ah, certainly do, ah, love you, grumble, growl.'*

His nickname was daddy bear, my mom's nickname was momma bear, and we were the ones eating Goldilocks.

Sometimes, he wore sunglasses. Oh, and his reading glasses. Those were certainly stylish. They were from the 80s, big, square, rounded bifocals. He'd wear them when he was reading the newspaper.

Chapter Five

Burried Alive

During the time his life was about to be over, Dad had these big, old, magnifying glass things. They looked like welding glasses but were for something else. He looked like Albert Einstein. He certainly would look more like him if Albert Einstein had a beard. They'd probably get along great. Two, one-of-a-kind men.

He kept himself clean for the most part. Some would say he had OCD, obsessive-compulsive disorder. He brushed his teeth and took showers more than a normal person would.

When we didn't have running water and electricity, he'd go diving in the pond, just in his skimmies.

Once, I remember, he chased Mom up the hill, and she locked him out.

"I got leeches on me. Get them off of me now! I mean it, now!" He growled frantically.

He chased my mom up the hill and into the sliding glass door. She locked him out.

So, he turned to me and said, "Baby girl, would you please get these leeches off me?"

"Sure thing, Daddy," I answered, happy to oblige.

He definitely didn't like my mom for some reason, but he loved me! The best part of it was that I was his number one girl!

Once, like always, Dad went missing. We couldn't find him. We looked everywhere, flipped the whole house up, and looked around the house too. Like outside and inside. Up and down. Round and round. In the bathroom, the kitchen, all three rooms, and the living room. Then outside. Under the house, around the house, up the driveway, and on the other property. Nothing. No dad anywhere.

But then, there was a rustle in the woods and bushes.

"There's Dad! We found him!" I clapped.

A 5-foot 11-inch-tall man, muddy from head to toe, emerged from the bushes.

"Where'd you go?" My mom asked.

"I went hunting. I looked all around and found what I was looking for." He answered.

Then he reached out his grubby hand, and in it was a rabbit.

"Got dinner for us. Yum. Fix up a fire, and we'll eat some rabbit. Fresh straight from the neck of the woods." He gleamed.

With mud all over his face and body, he handed my mom the *'fresh meat.'*

Then, he went inside and hopped in the shower, clothes and everything. "Awe, a cold shower for the army boy," he said. And he washed off. Throwing his wet clothes out of the cold shower and piled them up outside the shower curtain.

Living in the woods had its perks, and then there was the mud. The mud was always somewhere.

On me, on my sister, on my mom, and mostly on the grizzly bear, my dad.

Living with a Vietnam veteran was always full of surprises, and not a day went by boring. He'd definitely keep you busy plus entertained.

"Hey, you over there!" Dad exclaimed. "The tippy top of the mountain, young general."

I went along. "Yes, sir! That's the tip of the iceberg, young captain."

"Yeah, that is, and I see something on top of it." We kept going.

"This is it." We'd go on for hours, letting our minds and imaginations run. Yep, that was Dad and I.

He would let me have so much fun. That's why I'm so blunt and love to be the center of attention.

"That's it. Where's my runner-up, Leina bug?"

"There she blows. The one and the only! Leina bug!" I said.

Then Leina would join us. She was still just three at the time, but she was always included if she was around.

I was lucky to have the two of them. An awesome dad and a great sidekick. The loves of my life.

My seizure did me in the past twenty years, but now thinking back, it wasn't all bad. I wish I could've lived it before my dad passed away, but I didn't get the pleasure of that.

I think about Anabella now. She has a baby boy that you could die for. He's a little monster and gives her a hard time.

I can't wait to see them this summer and play these role plays like dad, Anabella, and I used to play. It will be so much fun, and hopefully, it will bring back good memories for Anabella too.

I remember this one time when Dad buried me in the ground. The dirt filled the whole, with me in it. He left me out there for days.

He'd walk by, and I'd holler, "Am I done yet?"

"No, you still have a couple more hours."

"But, Dad--"

"Now that's extra time added onto your stay."

"But, Dad!"

"Nope. You're not getting out. I mean it. Now, shut up." He said.

My body hurt after the first day, but I still listened. He always knew the best.

"Dad, please. I promise I'll be good." I begged.

"You're in the hole for a reason," he answered. "You're cleansing yourself, and it's gonna payout in the end."

"But, Dad!"

"Now, shut up. You're getting on my nerves." Was his response.

"Okay, Dad." I finally resigned.

Then I started talking to myself. That's the best way to make time go by faster.

'So, how are you doing today?'

'I'm doing good. If Dad would let me out of this mess, I'd feel better.'

'So, brain, what are you doing today?'

'Nothing, huh?'

'You're just an old stupid brain for letting me get into this mess. Deep in a hole, that's where I am." downward smile on my face.'

'I hate this. Get me out of here!

'I could go run around, but he's always around somewhere."

"I heard that, little missy. An hour added on, just for that remark." Came Dad booming voice.

When I finally got out of the hole, Dad cleaned up my wounds and put pitch from the trees on them. Then, he sat me next to the fire that was burning in the wood stove.

All bandaged up, I felt a lot better. I healed after almost a week and felt so much better now that I was done with my healing ordeal. I actually felt refreshed and nourished. I can't believe I complained that much. I seriously felt stronger. Feeling worthy of a medal and a big fat gold star.

Now that I'm older, I'd probably do it again. Plant my butt right next to a tree and bury myself. But Dad's dead now, so I don't know what to do. He kept me going and gave me the patience to finish the job. Maybe music this time? That might work.

But still, to this day, I don't know why he put me in a hole, but I dare say that it wasn't one of the top ten things I want to do in life, especially not on my bucket list. And if it was, then I can say I've done it and cross it off now. Thank you,

Dad, for that one. I've gotten tougher, and never will I ever do that to my kid. Nope.

Another memory was catching tadpoles with my daddy. He made the catching feel like we were two scientists fetching for a new life. What a mind-opening fix. Two scientists on a roll to a new breakthrough.

Finding the ones with feet growing and heads attached. Catching them in glass jars. You know the mason jars that you can use to make jam and canned goods? Well, these jars are also good for catching tadpoles.

He showed me the algae and the green slime that was. Slimy, slick, green, and fun. Feeling the slick stuff and putting it in the jars was for good deeds. We would watch them grow, but that's not all we did.

We'd catch snakes and frogs too. Thank God the mason jars came with a lid, and we poked four holes on the top of the lid or through the lid. It was so much fun. I was like his little trooper. A tomboy, to be exact. *Miss smart ass*, as everyone else would call me.

Out to the water, I'd go doing what Dad taught me to do. Catch living things and keep them so that I can watch them grow and become new beings.

We'd even walk on our pond in the winter. It was fun. We do ice skating. But there's always a downside to things. I remember, one day, we went out, you know, playing on the ice, and Anabella's friend fell straight in the water. She hit a patch of thin ice, and the next thing we knew, she was inside.

We all panicked. But luckily, she did get out and was okay, but it was scary. We definitely had a scare.

In the summers, we'd go swimming in the pond and play all day in that thing.

"You guys hungry? I got food cooking." Dad would ask.

"No, Dad, we're having fun. We are not done playing." We would answer.

"Maybe later then."

"Yeah, Dad!" I would yell back.

Chapter Six

Anabelle

My earlier days consisted of taking care of Anabella, my sister. I raised her myself. My dad just handed her to me. So, everywhere I went, she was there. If she cried, I'd get told to take care of her this way.

I would be like, "Dad, come on!"

But he'd say, "Nope, you're gonna need to learn how one day. So here you go. Here's your own little daughter."

I'd do everything with her. Like keep her busy by telling her stories and making her laugh at stupid shit I'd come up with to make her giggle. While acting like I was in a circus or a ballet constructor, I'd fall or hurt myself, and she thought that was funny too. She was my all, and I was hers.

I'd do the dishes and just talk the whole time to keep her occupied and make things fun. My mom would come home, then say she couldn't handle it, and leave the next day. She was so jealous of me. She hated me.

All I wanted was a mom, and instead, I was one myself.

Daughter of a Veitnam Veteran

I'd daydream about it all the time with Anabella. It was like we'd put on a show of how she would be with me and how it would go, but all Anabella knew how to do was giggle or say, "Ga, ga!"

That wasn't very helpful, now, was it? But life goes on. Still, to this day, she won't admit that I raised her. But guess what? I did! I changed her, I bathed her, I even took baths with her. She was my right-hand man.

After my seizure happened, I lost a lot of my memory. During that time, I was really mean to her, and she was only five. I mean, she didn't deserve it.

She'd always say, "I hate that you had that seizure," but it was the truth.

I would take her stuff and make her not be like me. Which could've been hard on her. Always following me and always being with me.

"I'll give you whatever you want. Just be my friend. Please! Just be my friend. I really miss you." She would beg me.

"No, stop being like me! I hate you! Go away!" I would yell back.

Over time, when this kept happening, finally, she couldn't take it anymore. She toughened up and made friends at school, and loved being at school.

She was an honor student in a high-cap class, the intelligent group, that would meet up once a week and follow up on you. I mean, they taught her Spanish, and they made her feel really special.

I'd get 2s and 3s on my report card. Anabella would get straight 4s, so Dad would pay her for every grade she got that was a four. It wasn't fair to me, but I think God had his eye on her. I know she felt lost and didn't know why Momma and I were mad at her.

I would beat her down and tell her she couldn't be like this because I liked it. It is so sad to think about, to remember that. Now, every day, I pray and ask God to give her back to me. I just want to be her, to be able to spend time together. We're states away from each other, and I know that we'll probably never be close like that again.

I know Anabella hates me, but all I can do is try, right? God, it beats me up to know it's right there. We can play imagination land. We can!

Dad tried to help us get close, but what he did didn't work. I was too selfish and didn't give a damn at that time.

"I know you two girls need each other. God, I wish you would just work it all out!" He would exclaim.

My seizure put me in a coma. I was out of it for three days straight! I couldn't remember shit. And my parents never worked with me to get my head straight. I get flashbacks all the time of all those horrible memories. Like, I'm actually living them again, and it freaks me out really bad.

Once, my time to shine came. This one time, us scientists decided to enter into the school science fair. Dad and I were talking and trying to think of what we could make to display at this fantastic science fair.

Finally, he goes, "We're going to make a volcano! We are going to need paper-mâché, a balloon, a mason jar, baking soda, red dye, and vinegar. Also, flour and water for the newspaper strips to stick together."

And so, the ordeal began. We first blew up a balloon and put it into the center of a square piece of plywood. Then we mixed up flour and water until its texture was like glue. Then we ripped strips of newspaper, put them in the mixture, and laid them one by one on the balloon.

We placed the strips horizontally over the balloon so it looked like a mountain, doing it over and over again. Then, we placed another layer of Papier-mâché over the last layer and did this three times. Then, we let the mountain of newspaper and glue, like a mixture of flour and water, sit until it became dry.

After that, we put two more layers on and let those dry too. When it finished drying, we popped the balloon and put a mason jar in where the balloon was. Finally, we touched it up with some paint. We painted it to look like the mountain had snow on it. Then it was finished! All that work went to use.

The next day, we took it to the science fair, and it was a hit! We let it go off! Volcano lava, come out and play! We put the vinegar, red food coloring, and baking soda into the mason jar. It was a chemical reaction!

Blam! Bam!

We won first prize and were on the front page of the newspaper. It was a hit.

"Thank you, Dad. You made me happy! Not every kid can say they built and won a project at the science fair with their dad. Noone." I hugged my father.

Now I can say that I had a blast building and setting off that volcano! I can't believe we won first place! See, my dad might have PTSD, but hey, he still was an amazing dad!

Somas or Carisoprodol is used short-term to treat muscle pain and discomfort. It is usually used along with rest, physical therapy, and other treatments. It works by helping to relax the muscles. But when taken by the handfuls, it's a zombie effect. My dad would fall asleep standing up. I mean, he was prescribed them, but it wasn't for this to happen. It was really hard seeing him this way.

He'd go out to his shop where the Harley was and rev the engine over and over again. One of the times, he took off while on somas. He crashed his bike and messed up his knees. It was terrible. The family had to pull together and go get him from a different state. I think it was Idaho, but we were from Shelton, Washington. That's a drive. Going across the country that far is really hard to do on a bike, and it definitely is a killer on Soma.

Other times, he'd be out of it, and I'd have to put him to bed. It was like I was his mommy. I remember this in my head. Times when I would put Anabella to bed, then tuck in Dad and give him a kiss on the forehead. God, I miss that. I think about Dad's stories all the time. Half the time, I can't even help it. I got the geniuses from my father. Flashbacks and PTSD.

I know that I will never be the same because of my childhood trauma. Never. Now I'm prescribed the medicine and relive my past every day. Thank you, Dad, for that!

In all cases, you spare the rod, and you spoil the child. I definitely remember my dad whipping the shit out of me. I remember Anabella, my little sister, crying, seeing me in so much pain.

"Daddy, no! Sorry, Daddy, I didn't mean to. It was Anabella who did it, not me. Please, Daddy, stop it!" He'd come down the hallway smacking the belt on the walls.

"Here, I'm coming. You best be ready."

"You girls are too quiet."

Smack, smack. Whip, whip. Would come the sound of the belt.

Daughter of a Veitnam Veteran

"No, Daddy, please!" I would beg.

We then showed up to school with welts all over our bodies. That was a big thing for me. No more whippings for me. He'd just slap the belt on the wall and make it snap by taking and making the belt fold in half and crack it. Cracking the whip.

Then he'd slap the bed just to scare us, and this went on until I had a seizure. It might have been that the whip was finally gone, but so were my memories.

Once, Mom had gone on one of her escapades. Dad had been cooking in the kitchen. He was making real food this time.

He said, "Now, girls, this is how you keep a kitchen. Nice and tight. Just like this. Rinse off all your dishes and then wash them with soap and hot water. Don't leave nasty mold and stuff under the towel that you drain the dishes on. Unlike your lazy, old mom who doesn't give a fuck about us. She'd let us all catch something and not care what she did. Follow me, and you'll get a good man one day."

He rinsed off the dishes, wiped down the counter, then laid the towel from his neck out on the counter and washed all the dishes.

I follow this recipe to this day. Many call it OCD. Many call it cleanliness. Whatever it is, it makes my man happy.

He says, "Listen here, girls, I'm going to show you how to cut a chicken up. I was in 4-H too, but I was doing the man part of it. First, you cut the bird straight down the middle. As I said earlier, there's a way to cut this whole chicken, and this is the recipe. Then cut the wings. Next, you cut the legs, and then you have your breast."

"Thanks, Dad, that'll make a good batch of chicken. Yum, chicken for dinner. The best. Especially handmade like that.! I cheered.

It was around midnight when Mom finally showed up. She was wasted and had been drinking what looked like a lot.

"Ah, you fucker! Why are the kids up?"

"Um, Mom, because you just woke us up," I said.

I mean, Dad had done this time and time again, showing up drunk. But this one time my mom did it, it really pissed me off. Dad's working all night and day, taking care of Anabella and me. He had reason to be drunk. Mom didn't.

Daughter of a Veitnam Veteran

Dad was all sweet to her and kindly put her to bed. Nice and cozy, she became.

"It feels good to get wasted sometimes, doesn't it? Leaving me and the kids at home to fend for ourselves. How selfish. Now go to bed, honey. We'll most likely see you in the morning. You'll have a hangover. Nighty, night."

See, Dad had been getting drunk, but we were always with him. She gets drunk and comes home for the first time in a long time. So, yeah, I was pissed. Wouldn't you be? You have to get drunk to be present in your house? To be with your family, your husband, and your kids? Why was it okay for her to drink? Well, at least, that's how I felt. No drinking, and especially not so much to get drunk. Not okay in my book. How selfish was that?

In the morning, we all surrounded her with love and kisses, but she had to leave again because it was too much for her to handle. I guess love and kisses didn't have a place in her book. So, no matter how much we begged, it didn't matter. She still left us again to fend for ourselves.

"Daddy, please say a prayer with us." We would request him.

"Yes, baby girls." He'd always say.

"Dear heavenly father, thank you for this day, and bless my girls as they sleep." My dad would start off our prayers every night. "Watch over them as they sleep. Please, forgive us for our sins. Thank you for this day. Thank you for my daughters. Please, let them have sweet dreams about you and heaven. In Jesus's name, we pray. Amen." He'd finish.

This was every night. I mean, every night. He'd stand in the hallway of the three rooms and say this prayer. We'd both finish with, "Will you please shut the door, Daddy? Just leave it open a crack."

He was a devoted father. He'd do anything his girls asked him to. Even if he didn't want to.

Chapter Seven

The Seizure

Having a seizure saved my life. It was from blunt force trauma. A lot of that came from the episodes I had with both parents. And seeing all the shit a little girl shouldn't have been seeing. My mom had been an addict, and so was my dad. My dad from the war, and my mom from her childhood. They were both the same, yet so different in so many ways.

I remember getting slapped in the face by my mom. That is the last memory I had until I woke up in the hospital with my dad praying at my side. I was in a coma for three days, and it really messed with my dad's head.

Seeing his tough little girl lying there with nothing going on in her poor little head. That changed him.

"I'm hanging up my guns for you, my precious baby girl. There's nothing stopping me from this change. I promise you a good life, baby girl. You're my world. Just don't go out on me like that again. I never let a soldier down. Never! You are Daddy's world! We were troupers, a team. We never fall down. No, not us!" He ranted the second I woke up.

After that day, my life would've changed.

"Nobody is allowed to hit my little girl's head. Nobody can hurt her! Ever!" He ordered.

I stayed with the duty that watched over us kids while playing in the recess yard. She became one of my best friends.

There were actually two duties, and I stayed right by their side. Duty Mrs. Caddy and Miss Tammey. They always had an eye on me., always watching me like a hawk.

My mom became my friend and kept me home, and took care of me. She would bring me an aspirin and my medications so I wouldn't have a seizure. I took Tegretol and had to take it twice a day.

My dad went out, working on his cars with Charlie, my uncle. Then he got a huge settlement from the V.A. veterans assistance program. Life got good after that.

My first time getting a really nice pair of shoes. It felt amazing! But I didn't get them. Instead, I got an Adidas jacket, and it was a hit.

"Where did you get that jacket?" The boy I liked asked me.

"From big 5. I might have wanted Nike shoes, but I saw this jacket. Thank you for asking." I answered shyly.

It was so nice to finally fit in with the other kids. We lived off of free clothing banks and Walmart before that, and I'd get made fun of.

Plus, I kept getting lice, so I was the bug girl. But no one dared call me that. My dad would make them pay if they did.

Then we got a 1998 special edition Harley Davidson with maroon and tan markings. It was beautiful. We played on it and took pictures of us playing on it. It was cool.

When Dad pulled up on the Harley, it was a big day! He now had a bike to go with the other bike riders, all Harley owners. He went everywhere on that bike. He went to Sturgis, Nevada, Reno, and Idaho, even South Dakota. That was his pride and joy.

Mom and Dad were happy too. They started spending time with each other again. It was like they finally got to bond again, and it was over a bike. They became best friends, traveling the States together.

Going riding on it for the first time was off the Richter scale. It was finally my turn. I was about eight or nine, riding on the front of the bike. Then around ten, I rode about forty miles on the back, from our house all the way to the ocean. Yep, ocean shores.

Once we were riding to the ocean, Dad reached back and asked, "How are we doing?" He would always check up on me.

"Are you still comfortable?" He asked.

"Yeah, Daddy, I'm fine," I responded.

"Your butt hurts? It's a long ride." He asked, still concerned.

Then we stopped at the store, and indeed, my butt was hurting.

Mom had followed us in the car, packed with all our ocean gear. She came up to me.

"Your butt hurts?" She asked.

"Yes, it does." I laughed.

"Awe, well, come on, we still got about twenty miles to go." Mom said.

"Man, you should have seen it. When we rode all the way down to South Dakota, I kept yelling for your father to stop because my butt needed a rest." She laughed.

My mom was the most outgoing and fun to be around person. When she was around, it was always amazing. I think that's why I missed her so much when she was gone.

My parents got married in Reno and did a quick marriage instead of a show wedding. More romantic, I think.

On our way to the bus every morning, we had lectures with Dad. It all seems funny now as I look back.

I was always yelling, "Stop lecturing us, Dad!"

'Why me?' I would think.

He'd start with, "You know, when I was a kid, it was different. You have to get good grades. Boys are trouble. Now don't be faking sick."

You know the things not to do and to do. I always thought it was him just talking, yelling, "Stop lecturing me. dad!"

That was so stupid of me. I look back and can't believe that none of it stuck. I know he said more, but all I was worried about was myself. I mean, come on.

Do you know what the worst thing is? That he was always right.

Once, I got stuck on the woodshed.

"Help, Dad! Help! I'm stuck on top of the roof." I yelled from the top of the woodshed. "There's a ladder and everything, but I can't get down!"

Dad scurried out of the house. "How did you get on top of there? You can get down." He boomed.

Yep, that's me. The adventurous Leiloni, the superhero.

'Hmm. Where do we go today? I know the brink of the shed of wood. That's a good idea! Why not?'

Today was just the day that the superwoman got stuck up high. Very smart. Well, at least that's a doozy. A big time in my life.

"You can get down from there." Came dad's voice.

I started crying and said, "No, it's too high. I can't."

I tried to use the ladder, but then I looked down and got dizzy. Going back to the top of the woodshed, I started crying even more.

"Daddy, help me, please! I can't get down." I pleaded.

"Come on, baby girl, you can do it," Dad responded. "I know you can make it. You got up there, so I know you can make it down. Just do it the way you did when you got up there, and you will be fine."

But me being me, I refused and kept crying.

Finally, Dad gave up trying to convince me, climbed the ladder, and grabbed me.

"Thank you, Daddy. I got scared." I said.

"No problem, baby girl. Just don't do it again. If you do it again, I'm just going to let you figure it out next time."

"Okay, Daddy," I answered and gave him a hug.

Corresponding together, we then left that damn woodshed. I learned my lesson for that day. Never again, ever, nope, not again.

See, I was raised in the woods, and my parents just let me do whatever I wanted. I'd be outside for hours, playing on the trees that had fallen, climbing on the ones that were still standing, making the trees into sea horses, balance beams, making the land my play yard, going up and down the tall trees and logs that were down. It was a lot of fun. The land of the free, beautiful land, the sky tree, and all kinds of different imaginary lands that my mind would release. Fun times.

Lucky me! Coming across an option like this to have the woods to play in, going on for miles, with nothing but trees, was like winning the lottery. The world that I grew up in was the world of fiction.

Anabella, my little sister, made up *HeartLand* as her playland, clear on the other side of the yard. So, I was on the east, and she was on the west, opening our eyes to the tree world.

Dad would come to play with us sometimes. He was the one to make up our land names by showing us the world Astore.

"See, kids, this is the opportunity of a lifetime, the world at your fingertips. Call it what you want, but it's our land of the free, the option of a tree. Wisdom of life. The life around that loves to be." Dad would say. He loved to rhyme, and it made so much more sense when he did.

Chapter Eight

The Mitsubishi

Dad gave me a set of keys to an old vehicle he had set up. He said, "Now, don't go on any of the main roads. Stay in the back forty."

So, I took the keys and went on my way. I could just barely touch the pedal, and it was a stick!

I had ridden on Dad's lap as an infant, steering the wheel for him to go down the old dirt road we lived on until we got home.

Then one day, he said, "It's time for you to learn how to drive! Get in the driver's seat."

We switched places, and he said, "Now push on the pedal to the left and make sure it's all the way to the ground. Then turn the key on."

So, I turned the key on and pushed the pedal all the way to the floorboard.

Vroom, Vroom! Went the car.

"Now, put the car in gear. You got to take your hand and put it on the stick shift. Put it all the way up and to the left." Dad instructed me.

I did as he told me.

"Now push in the gas pedal just a little. Now slowly let off the clutch."

Slowly, lifting my foot off the clutch, I let a little gas, and *bam, bang, bam, bam.* The car went forward, then it died.

"Shit, Dad, I can't do this."

"Yes, you can. Now do it again. Turn the key back on to make sure your clutch is in."

"Okay, Dad. Trying it again. Pushing in the clutch and turning the key."

I did, and the car started again.

"Now, try it again. Make sure it's the first." Dad said.

"Okay, Dad," I answered, shifting the gear stick first and making sure it was in the right place. Dad helped me.

"Okay, now give it a little gas and let the clutch loose slowly."

Vroom, vroom, and away we went. We got up to about 15mph.

"Now shift it into second. Straight down. Put in the clutch and let her rip." Dad continued with the instructions.

Putting my foot down on the clutch again, I slipped the gear shift into second, straight down, just like Dad said.

"Now we're cruising! I like this!" Dad said with glee.

"Dad, I did it! I can drive now! Thank you, Daddy." I exclaimed happily.

After that, I drove all over hell and back. Driving on the back roads down, new roads, different scenery, every time I went back in the back forty.

Then, one day, Dad and I were driving, and he said, "We're going to take a shortcut. Turn here, and I'll show you the other backwoods. The 800 line."

Taking the turn, we got to the road with a yellow gate. It was open. It was hunting season. They were all open.

"Yeah. Now this is the 800 line. We can go all the way up a mountain or go out to Skoke Valley. Let's go straight, and we'll come out and down the mountain. We'll pass by the gravel yard. You'll see it. This is a good time, driving out here. I remember when I was working as a logger. I cut down trees and drove them all over the place out here. We go around a corner, and there we have it, the gravel yard. They store their gravel to keep the roads up and tight and nice and clean. No bumps or bruises there." Dad explains.

We drive for about five more minutes and then comes a steep windy road down the hillside. We were climbing down a steep hill with windy corners.

"Let's count the corners. One, two, three…twenty-seven corners."

Counting our way down the side of the hill, we finally got to the bottom.

"Hey, we're in Skoke Valley. Let's see how much the river has flooded. Hope we can make it through." Dad mumbled.

"I hope so, too," I said, venturing around the corner.

"Oh, that's the fish hatchery. The fish might be swimming. Take this right, and we'll see what's going on down this road. How high is the water line, Leius?"

As we drove, we came up on our first water over the roadway. "Oh, well, that's not too bad. Go on, drive through it." He said after I gave him a look.

'Scared we won't make it? I bet we will. Take it nice and easy.'

Getting through the water, I chanted to myself,

"We're done with the first one."

It was about halfway up the tires on the car the whole way through. Driving along, here comes another one.

"Oh, shit, I don't think we're going to make it through this one. Look at the water line. It is two feet above ground level. No way will we make that one. We'd probably float away, and the car would become a boat." Dad said.

So, we got back in the car and turned around.

"Back up the hillside and around the corner to the house. That was shitty. I wanted to show you more, but maybe another time. Now you can drive out this way and even make it to the Skoke." Dad sighed.

"Cool, Dad. That was awesome!" I smiled, taking in everything that I just learned. It was all a great experience.

"I love you, baby girl!" He exclaimed.

"I love you too, Dad," I answered.

We finished off the day by taking the back roads home.

Dad always let off a growl when he talked, mumbling words of great truth and value to you. He made it so you had to listen really well.

He'd say *fucker,* and it'd be *fuck-a-rr, growl, grumble.* His favorite words were, "God, damn it," and, "I'm a goner."

Because of this, my mom would call him, *'I'm a goner.'*

It was funny, but it was his speech and his wording that kept you listening. He'd tell stories about when he was a kid when we were on drives and show us who, what, and where he worked.

"Oh, Leius, I worked picking berries when I was your age. I used to pick brushes too. But those Mexicans, man, they stole all our jobs. A quick way to save your day brush picking." He'd always bitch.

Even when he aged, he looked very handsome. But he shrunk, got beaten up, you know, the decline of age process.

"God, that smells good! What is that tasty smell? Oh, I know, it's Daddy's cooking! Yay! The best of the best! What is it, I wonder? I think it smells like chicken! Fried chicken! Homemade, all-around secret recipe. Yum! Do you know what the secret recipe is? It's some good old biker love! Only get that when you can. No one could even rise up against it." I cheered Daddy as he cooked.

That cooking was always good. He'd fry up a whole chicken. He even showed me the real way of making some homemade chicken.

"You got to cut the chicken in a special way." He said.

This was because of what he was taught in 4-H. He'd tell stories about the fair and having to know how to butcher a chicken. So, he showed me and everyone else that would listen or wanted to have his recipe. It took some real effort. Lots of paying attention to how things were made in this house. But that's not all. He'd make a badass turkey on

Thanksgiving and his homemade stuffing. Now that was a pretty harsh way of making it, but you couldn't tell the gizzards were in it.

Yep, he cooked down the insides and cut just a little from everything, and through that, in the pot of dressing. It all got eaten up and was enjoyed.

His grill time was also fun. He'd grill up a flank steak, and my nephews could smell that from a mile away. I mean, right in the middle.

"What's that, Grandpa?" They would ask.

"Some of the grandpa's famous steak. You want some?" Dad would ask. And that was the end of that.

I remember Dad even got a Mitsubishi.

Man, that Mitsubishi was his hot rod. He loved showing me how it could handle the corners. The corners were out by our house. The way to Matlock Washington going from our house to the good old Matlock, home of the free! For sure!

There were these corners that were pretty rounded. We would go 60 mph around them.

Daughter of a Veitnam Veteran

He said, "Now, Layus, look at how I'm handling this corner. You got to never press your brakes but hug the corners like so. Then press the gas as you're rounding the corner. Look how well we're handling this bitch. That's how you drive."

Then, on our way back home, he handed me the keys and said, "Now, it's your turn. Show me how you handle those corners."

So, I got into the Mitsubishi and started my journey to the house, coming up on the corners, "Now, remember what I showed you. Take that corner, now hug it." As we round the corner, I did a pretty good job!

"Now press on the gas as you round this baby girl." He grumbled. I was so proud after I did it.

"Hey, now that's how you do it, baby girl. Remember to always do it as I showed you. *Never* push on the brakes!"

Driving in the Mitsubishi was fantastic! As loud as it could go, squeaking wheels and revving the engine, music blasting, my stuff, of course. Dad even started to sing it with Anabella and me. It was priceless. A biker guy singing hip-hop and rap was pretty cool. I mean, he was from the sixties, so it's rare to find such a thing. I mean, if you're not black.

79

Nothing against blacks, but those bikers, loved their hippy music and classic rock.

See, we lived down a dirt road, and in the summer, it'd kick up dust from the cars driving over it. That just made the car dusty as hell.

So, Dad would pamper his hot rod and would, give it baths and keep her clean. She was his baby. No scratches, no nothing on this car made it sparkle in the light. It was squeaky clean.

I also remember how Dad always sang songs in the morning. It was cute. His songs consisted of *'Oscar, Meyer, wiener,' 'this is my rifle, this is my gun,'* and a lot of other ones. He'd be making mickey mouse pancakes and singing them loud as hell.

"Dad shut up! Keep it down in there. I'm trying to watch the television." I'd yell then, but now, I look at it as a good memory. I would probably do the same for my kids. It might have been annoying to deal with, but it is pretty funny to reminisce about later.

I want my kids to have these beautiful memories.

Chapter Nine

The Cool Parents

I remember Mom and dad were running a celebrate recovery group at our church. We met all kinds of people just like us. It was really nice and very cleansing. They would open up with the serenity prayer.

"God, grant me the serenity to accept the things that I can and cannot change. The courage to change the things I can and the wisdom to know the difference."

These words to a recovering addict are life-changing and have quite a strong hold. They are a game changer.

Some of the people we met came from a really long road of using. They came to stay with the church and the program. It was awesome to watch. My mom and dad led the group, but they had help, too, from some of the church people.

Both my parents stayed clean for almost twelve years. In that time frame, a lot had happened. We'd do church outings and have potlucks. It was a lot of fun! My dad changed dramatically. He would pray at dinner, speak at church, and become an usher there too.

His whole persona changed. We would have friends over, and they'd go to church with us. Everyone would go with us. My dad was so loving and kind you wouldn't even believe it. The way he did everything and the way he looked so scary, like a badass biker, made it even better. He'd even use his bike and ride it to church. It just made him tougher. It felt unreal, too good to be true.

The program brought bikers in too. Being a recovering addict has its ups and downs. You may be clean and sober, but you always have that want to do drugs or drink alcohol in the back of your head. Plus, seeing others using addicts and hanging out with them can cause a relapse if they're not in the program.

If they are in the program, they're bad to hang out with. They can persuade you to drink and relapse by putting drugs around you. That's what happened to my mom. She started to use it again because she saw other people using it and didn't want to be an outcast. So, she picked it up again.

My Mom had a daughter from someone else too. Mom and Dad said yes to my dad's stepdaughter to stay in the trailer outside.

She had been a really bad alcoholic and a drug user My mom, being a recovering addict, slipped up and started drinking. She hadn't come home and was missing. Yet again, like when I was a child.

So, Dad, Anabella, and I went on a witch hunt. We found her down at *"The Loggers Bar and Grill,"* drunker than a skunk. It was just the tip of the iceberg. My dad fought for her to get clean and sober again and again but didn't succeed.

Her *use* was the start of my dad's *use*, and Dad went all out when he started up his addiction too.

"Well, the kids are old enough now, so why not? It won't hurt them."

That was what Dad thought and even said it out loud. They didn't even think about what they had just done and the road that they put us on. It was a roller coaster ride from hell.

Being older didn't change a thing. My family had been on the road from hell in the beginning, and it was ten times worse, so I guess I can't bitch. It's just how they could handle life on life's terms, I guess.

They had a disease called alcoholism. Some people die from it every day or a couple of hours, I don't know exactly, but people die from it. It's no joke.

Mom ended up dying from alcohol. She had cirrhosis of the liver and wouldn't stop drinking even on her deathbed. It killed my dad to see and go through it. He loved her so much. It was sad to watch. She went from radiant to pickled. Her skin turned yellow, and the same happened to her eyes. *She became yellow all over.*

Sleeping in bed with mom and dad. Now, that was just difficult. I still remember the hard floor and the end of the bed.

Dad always said, "And they stayed in our bed until they were nine and ten years old."

We totally ruined their sex life, and we were too old to sleep with them. But they were too loving to stop us from being in their bedroom. Who cares if we ruin their sex life. They loved us.

So, it started off with bad dreams. I remember it.

"Daddy, I had a nightmare." My sister and I would say.

"Awe, baby, come lay down with me and cuddle." Dad would say.

"Okay, Daddy, I'm scared. Momma, I love you. Please, can we cuddle?"

"It's okay. Everybody has nightmares." Were mom's caring words.

One of our other excuses was, "Daddy, I'm scared."

So, of course, I was scared every night and ended up sleeping on the floor of Dad's room. This would flip-flop and go from the bedroom floor to the bed. I would cuddle with Mom and then cuddle with Dad.

I remember Dad floating on the water on two garbage bags full of weed. What a guy! Who do you know that would do something like this? I know my daddy sure did.

He was a big pothead. Way before weed was legal. Marijuana, pot, the kind, and Ganja. All the names of that beautiful flower. The way it smells is like paradise. I don't like to smoke, but a lot of people do.

Dad's friends say, "He liked to smoke. He was the one to get it from."

So, Dad knew a lot of people. If you know what I mean.

He'd tell us stories about his drug expeditions, and he had some pretty good ones. Reminiscing and hallucinating happily to himself. He'd put himself in a vegetative state. It was cool, and I thought my dad was the coolest. Not everybody has a hippy dad like that. They might do now, but not in my generation.

See, Dad was older than all the other kids. Dad and I hated it until I got older. Then I was the cool girl that had badass, laid-back parents. They'd let all the kids come over and get wasted at our house, out in the woods.

We were all partying out there. All the time.

"What's up? Can I come out? I got a bottle." Kids would call me and say.

"Yeah, come out. I'm totally open to some free liquor and a good time. Bring out some good stuff, and we'll get wasted together." Was always my reply, you know?

It was so much fun, and I had a lot of parties and get-togethers at that house. My house was *the house*, as I call it now.

Daughter of a Veitnam Veteran

God, I had gangster ass parents, didn't I? Having parties and being loud while they sat in the back room. The parties would get crazy too. I mean loud, and there were lots of fights. The hatchet even came out once. Drugs would sometimes come out, but it was mostly all alcohol. Thank God, no one ever called the cops.

That's for sure.

See, living in the woods, not like any woods, had its advantages too. Down a dirt road, like a mile, and with no close neighbors, like I said. Well, at the time. That was a big plus.

Some of the neighbors down the road would come over, and that would get crazy too. The neighbors were all veterans of some kind of war, and their kids would show up too.

Even a cop's son came once. Now that was a close one. We almost got busted.

Thank God that he never said anything. My parents would have been shut out of luck, if you know what I mean.

"Get a cup! Come on, baby girl, dads waiting to get his bath." I heard Mom yell.

So, what did I do?

I grabbed a big ass glass and brought it to my mom. She loved pampering people. It was always giving you a bath, her bath, and, of course, my favorite, Dad's bath time.

Giving Dad his bubble baths with Mom was so much fun because you'd get Dad's hair with a glass of bubble water, and he'd look like a wet bear or dog.

Getting him into a bath was like pulling a tooth from a child. It was so hard because he thought it was a lady's thing. He'd only take a bath if it was from the kids and me. Enjoying getting a bath from us is what he'd do.

Even though it was so rarely done, he was happy to get one. Dad was like a kid hiding his junk in the bubbles.

It was pretty funny. It's not like we even cared. We were just little then. Didn't even know what it was.

We'd get him in the bath, then come in because of this. Then we'd get his beard and hair wet, soap him up, and run out when we dipped him. So, there was no seeing him completely naked. It was a moral thing, I guess. Plus, it was a laughing time, a lady screaming because she had lost her towel.

Daughter of a Veitnam Veteran

The good memories, the things you'd add to your journal or tell a tale about later on in life. My dad was super cool and very proper. His mom raised him this way, and his grandpa did, too, at that. My dad, certainly, was a gentleman.

When Teresa died, it was heart-dropping. The first time I ever saw my veteran daddy cry. He was the toughest, and it was hard to watch. It brought down his spirits. He changed after that and never was the same again. That was his oldest daughter, and she was his world.

They spent a lot of time together, and that time they had shared really made him want to live. I hadn't thought that it was a thing until Dad started to die right in front of me.

I had just gotten back from stealing the car and heading halfway around the country.

I felt so bad and still do to this day. The feeling of sadness, from my point of view, was more remorseful than I can even put into words.

He went to the funeral, and they had a big one for her and buried her in a casket. He was given the necklace that my sister had been wearing when she died. I took it and put it on. I wore it because I wanted to be closer to her.

When I was wearing it, I did feel close to her. I wanted to bring joy to the consortium of life and death. One sister to another. You know, show Dad that I could be like her, but I was too young to understand that the way people mourn is way different in all aspects of death in a certain way. It took me losing my mom to understand. That was really hard on me.

The feelings you get and the ups and downs of death itself, wishing never to have this bless our house again. No more mourning! No more!

Why does death happen anyways? Can we be together on the other side? Or is it just rebirth to someone or something that has nothing to do with who you were before?

Thinking about it, I really don't know.

Trying to be the one that's there for you in all the ways that can be, from me, a child only fourteen years of age, never having lost something that special and seeing someone in that state is hard.

Now, I look back, and I wish that I could've done better. Walking in her footsteps as if she were still there, looking back and thinking I could have never replaced her to make him happy.

I mean, I could have tried harder, and I did. I sure did. But I wasn't strong enough for Dad. Never as beautiful as her. God, if only. Now in the way of the bible, let them be together. Let them finally be peace and joy. Let there be manifestations and strengths in their every footstep.

But we did bond on many other levels though. Dad would walk through the stores with me, we would shop and spend quality time together. It definitely was always good times. He'd just walk up and down the aisle with me. I'd be in the middle of all the clothes, showing Dad the outfits, and I'd say, "This is cute!"

"Are you sure you are going to wear it?" He would as me.

"Yeah, Dad. It's just my type." I would respond.

"Okay, then. Do your shopping. Is that all you're going to get?" He'd ask.

"No, Dad, I'm still looking." I'd reply.

"Well, go look then." Was his grumbling growl.

I never worried about the price because he told me not to worry about how much it cost.

"Just have some fun!" Was what he would tell me.

So, we'd walk out with three hundred dollar worth of clothes and have a heyday going to get shoes. It was so much fun, but things do come to an end. Sometimes quickly and sometimes slowly.

Eventually, my mom got sick. She contracted liver sclerosis but still wouldn't quit drinking. It was a slow, painful death, and it really got to me. Seeing her like that made me turn to drugs. I wanted to die slowly with her. She had become my best friend and a really good mom.

All my friends called her Mimi or Mom. Because she became that figure in their life too. It's a really long story about her and her addiction.

It also really messed with my dad's head. He couldn't bear it. It killed him at the same time. But Mom didn't care. She just wanted to stay drunk. Watching all this really killed not only him but me too. Watching your dad and mom die together really beats up an eighteen-year-old and her baby sister too.

Daughter of a Veitnam Veteran

Turning to drugs wasn't the greatest idea, but we did. We all had our choice of drug. Anabella's was perks, my dad's was alcohol, and mine was meth. It killed us but also put a band-aid on the pain for a little bit. We were all in our own prison.

Dad went through girlfriend after girlfriend until he landed on one who stayed. She was a story to tell, but I loved her anyway. The others were crazy as hell and drunks, just like my mom. They all acted like my mom and dad did when they first got together. It was a flashback city.

My dad had guns too. Oh man, I remember being so scared of him, nothing like you'd ever imagine. The worst part was he could smell the fear on me. That made me even worse.

The way I felt after my mom died was the first time I ever felt like that in my entire life.

I felt so scared that Dad was really going to hurt me like he hurt my mom because I wasn't his little bear anymore. I now felt like the enemy.

Running away from him and having him chase me with that look in his eyes, it scared me to death.

Leiloni Lynn Caughell-Simpson

Fire of ambers, red flames, and the taste for enemy flesh—scary—that's what it felt like. It wasn't what I or any daughter would ever expect their father to look at them like.

I mean, he had those looks before, but nope, not at me, no way. Then it happens, and you remember the ones who had lost their lives to this guy. God, if only I knew. Well, guess what? I found out.

My mom died, and we all faded away to our own addictions. My sister did too, but she graduated top of her class and was the valedictorian. I was and still am so proud of her.

I even wrote a song for her, my sister.

My baby, baby, sissy; My little, little, missy.

Now head off to college with this I pledge.

I give my heart to you to be a better me.

My baby, baby, sissy; My little, little, missy, now that mom is gone,

I don't know what's going on, but keep your head up.

To be a better me, my baby, baby, sissy; My little, little, missy, yeah!

Daughter of a Veitnam Veteran

I wrote that for her from the depth of my heart. Because even though she didn't show, I know she struggled too, just the same as me. It's a sad story, but after my mom's passing, we all changed.

Chapter Ten

My Dad, My Hero!

My dad didn't want to let his soldier down, so he stepped right into the hurricane that I let off. He grabbed me with both hands, and we went toe to toe with the devil.

Things would change very quickly, and sometimes it would just hit like a tornado. First, he got with his stepdaughter from a previous marriage. She was so crazy and drunk all the time. She never quit, and to top it all off, she just kept him drunk too. So, time after time, she ended up turning him into a terribly drunk alcoholic.

He was downing a half gallon every two days. They would fight, and they would have a good time too. It was all a haze. Dad would shoot out the lights and the T.V. There were gunshots from all over the place. We would have to have my brother and his wife come over when he had the gun. They would calm him down by talking to him and then slowly getting the gun out of his hands.

See, he wasn't supposed to have guns, but he did anyway. He'd shake his head and let his hair flow in the wind like he was a supermodel or something. It was cute yet scary. I loved him so much, but I was so scared of him too. He got a kick out of that. It wasn't funny, but he thought it was.

Diana was the next woman he went through. She was crazier than the last. And God, she was crazy. She got Dad to start doing meth. That made us see another side to Dad. Man, it was so sad.

Then, like the cherry on top, she moved her crazy ass son in, and they tag-teamed me. One was holding me down, and the other was punching me in the nose. A clear shot right to the nose. It was so bad. I still have a scar on my nose because of the situation that took place. It's something that never lets me forget what happened and what I went through.

They drove like a bat out of hell! Once, I remember, it was snowing, and we were out in the Toyota four runner. The new Toyota, not the one we had forever.

Brice, Diana's son, was sitting in the back seat with me. Dad and Diana were wasted and still drinking.

Dad stopped so we could go pee.

"Go on, girls, do your dirty work. Don't let that snow get up your butt." He grumbled to himself.

We did, but before I got done, Diana ran back in the Toyota four runner and said, "Go, go!"

And they left me and Brian standing there in the cold, snowy hillside. I was frozen by the time they came around the back.

"Get in. We must have forgotten about you. Sorry." They said and laughed their asses off.

"Why'd you leave us, Dad? That wasn't very nice, and it's cold out. Assholes." I answered, quite mad.

And that was our journey with Dad and Diana. Just to give you a quick outlook on their relationship and the fun we had too.

This other time, when my mom was still alive, we took the same journey. Out in the four runners, stomping those hills to pieces. It was a slow ass ride through the back forty.

The back was forty acres of nothing but logging roads. We lived right by them. They were about a quarter mile away from home, and you didn't even have to leave the dirt road.

We had been snow plowing, which was kind of just driving over the hills of the back forty. The gates were open, so we went on our journey down to Skoke, running over the snow, up and down, through this road, and that road, just having fun.

Suddenly, Dad decided to go up the mountain to the steel bridge.

Bump! Bump! Bump! The four runners ran up and down the bumpy road, straight up the slanted hilltop, through the potholes.

"Dang, that's a bumpy road." Dad hollered.

"It sure is, Pa." My mom said.

"It was fun, don't ya think?" He goes on with his hollers.

"Yeah, it sure is cool out here when it snows!" Mom gasped.

"Yeah, it is." That was my response.

"Why don't you get out and look over that edge. You can see the whole Skoke. Ain't it beautiful?" Dad says.

"Damn, this view is gorgeous. Man, I wish I had a camera." I whispered.

Looking over the ridge, I see the river, the trees, the rolling hillsides, and the beautiful section of earth's design cut out to make a scenery worth living for. The outlook of the place wins me over.

Well, finally, we get back into the forerunner and head on out. We drive aways and bam! We're at the steel bridge. There's snow all out and deep too. Mom and I had to go pee and she wanted to check out the scenery too. She pulled down her pants right in the middle of the road.

"No one is out here, but still, you better keep an eye out for me. I mean it. I don't want anybody seeing me pee. Would you, sissy." She said and then pulled down her pants all the way this time. She squatted in the middle of a snow—in the middle of the road.

Feeling naughty, I ran up and pushed her down in the snow, where she had just peed. Then ran my ass off.

I laughed, and Dad did too. It was priceless. This was how it was with Mom. But with Diana, it was definitely the worst. She consumed way too much alcohol and was always drunk. I mean, a horse would have alcohol poisoning, too, if it drank as much as they did.

Dad had gotten really tough on me the last couple of years I was with him. It was eye-opening and really mean at the same time. He'd make me catch the bus and walk anywhere that I needed to go. It was like he was preparing me for the future.

I'd walk miles into town and down to the lake house. We'd fight over heroin because I'd be sick from not having it. It was the worst time of my life, but it was during that time that we got close.

He'd take me with him to Tacoma, Washington, about two hours from home, and we'd talk and spend money freely. It was then that we bonded after a long time too.

The last place he took me, on the actual day he died, was to the dairy queen to get ice cream. We laughed and told jokes and had the time of our lives.

And I had no idea that it was going to be the last time I had fun with him, but I'm glad I did. It was fun!

God, I miss him. May the angels lead the way.

He died at the age of sixty-nine, and now I'm a single soldier on the run. It's hard to think that if I have a problem, I have to fix it myself, and he's not going to be there to help me. I mean, it's tough, though, that he won't be here to clean my mess.

Leiloni Lynn Caughell-Simpson

I wrote this song for him before he died.

I got a Vietnam vet under the weather.

Thank you to the soldiers, thank you to the soldiers,

Because I got a Vietnam veta under the weather.

Thank you to the soldiers, thank you to the soldiers,

There in and out.

Gotta shout to the moon in a lagoon,

I got a Vietnam vet under the weather.

Thank you to the soldiers cause I got a Vietnam veta under the weather.

Thank you with a shiver, a meat cleaver,

Cause I got a Vietnam veta under the weather.

Thank you to the soldiers, thank you to the soldiers, thank you to the soldiers.

The life that I lived and the things that I went through made me who I am today. It taught me to respect people that people have forgotten about. World War Two veterans, Vietnam veterans, Iraq and Afghanistan soldiers too, a desert storm veteran, even our elders.

How many elders out there get their doors held open for them? I know, for a pretty girl, you'd open the door for me, wouldn't you? So, why not for someone who looks different with a beard and a cane? Would you open the door for them?

I just think it's respectful and should be done. Being raised like that and all, to respect our wounded soldiers and grownups, too.

There are always lessons we can learn and things we can do to change the world.

By recognizing our surroundings, taking a look at the world from a different perspective, and learning from the mistakes that we have made, we can make a difference.

It starts small, and it starts with us. We should not worry about whether it's being done by others or not, but we should worry about ourselves and our own actions.

In a nutshell, we all have a story to tell. What's yours?

I'd like to personally thank all soldiers of foreign wars for serving in our country. I wish them all beautiful lives and beautiful skies forever and ever and a day!

Hopefully, this book helped you know that no one is perfect at raising their kids, even if they are on drugs, neither parent nor child at that. No one is god. People mess up, but you learn from that and move on.

I hope you liked my outlook on this.

Leiloni Cughell-Simpson

Thank You!

Daughter of a Veitnam Veteran

www.ingramcontent.com/pod-product-compliance
Lightning Source LLC
Chambersburg PA
CBHW021654120626
46545CB00002B/852